JERUSALEM
Arab Origin and Heritage

JERUSALEM
Arab Origin and Heritage

M. A. Aamiry

Longman

Longman Group Limited

London

*Associated companies, branches and representatives
throughout the world*

© Longman Group Ltd

First published 1978

British Library Cataloguing in Publication Data

Aamiry, M A
    Jerusalem.
    1. Civilization, Arab   2. Jerusalem – History
    I. Title
    956.94'4   DS109.9   77–30751

ISBN 0 582 78047 0

Phototypeset in V.I.P. Plantin by
Western Printing Services Ltd, Bristol
and printed in Great Britain by
The Pitman Press, Bath

Contents

Preface

This book deals with a single aspect of the early history of Jerusalem: its Arab origin and the continuity of the Arab race in the Holy City—as well as in the whole of Palestine. Many foreign writers, and indeed some Arabs too, commit a common error by suggesting that the Arabs inhabited Palestine only from the year AD 638, the beginning of Muslim rule. They ignore the fact that the Arabs, under various ancient tribal names, were the dominant inhabitants of the country from the beginning of its human habitation.

What the Muslim Arabs did in AD 638 was to put an end to the Roman occupation of Palestine, and of Jerusalem. The native inhabitants, Christian and pagan, were descended from the original Carmel Man of Palestine, and from the Semitic Arab tribes of Amorites, Canaanites, and others who had entered the land from Arabia in migratory waves. The Jebusites, who built Jerusalem, were a sub-group of the Canaanites.

The "Divine Promise" and the "Historical Right" claimed by the Zionists are of course scientifically untenable, and study shows that the Patriarchs never based their actions on such a promise, while Christians and Muslims claim similar promises.

Modern historical investigation, based on the findings of archaeology, shows that the Hebrews of the Old Testament were a limited group, that their rule in Jerusalem as a city-state was of short duration, that the city-states of Judaea and Samaria were two of many scattered throughout Palestine, and that Hebrew rule ended as many successive foreign invasions ended. The invasions by Hittites, Hyksos, Hurrians, Persians, Greeks, and Romans were generally more extensive and lasted longer.

In so short a book as this, one cannot mention every source consulted, but enough, I hope, has been cited to support the thesis. My larger book, written in Arabic but now being translated into English, quotes authorities, historical and archaeological, of a much wider provenance.

My thanks are due here to H. E. Sheikh A. El-Sayeh, former Minister of the Holy Places; to H. E. Sayed Ruhi El-Katib, Mayor of Arab Jerusalem expelled to Jordan; to Sayed Abdul-Rahman Bushnaq, member of the Jordan Academy; and to others who helped with the preparation of this book.

M. A. Aamiry

A Canaanite Family in Jericho, about 2000 BC
A high standard of civilisation had been attained seven centuries before the Hebrew invasion.

Chapter One

The Earliest Inhabitants
of Jerusalem

A book on Jerusalem may perhaps most usefully begin by explaining something of the people who first established the city. It will also be enlightening to look at the ancient relationship between Jerusalem itself and the neighbouring countries of Egypt, Lebanon, Syria, and Mesopotamia (modern Iraq); for the peoples of all these countries, from the time of their earliest settlements, ranged freely over the whole area, which was always regarded as a single region. Recent archaeological discoveries have confirmed the ethnic relationship between the peoples who lived here, in what is called the Fertile Crescent, and the nomadic tribes of the Arabian Peninsula. The Peninsula was the reservoir which supplied these countries with almost all their original inhabitants.

The Arabs of modern Palestine derive from the stock which, under various tribal names, inhabited these regions in prehistoric times. These names, for example Amorite and Canaanite, commonly denoted the areas where the tribes lived, and most were used as early as the third and second millennia BC. According to our present knowledge, it was probably the Jebusites, an offshoot of the Canaanites, who founded Jerusalem, in about the fourth or third millennium BC.

The people calling themselves Israelites appeared as recently as about 1300 BC[1], or even later,[2] and did not conquer Jerusalem until approximately 1000 BC. They established a kingdom which, under David and Solomon, lasted for a mere seventy years. It was then divided into two, one of which broke up within two centuries and

1

the other within three and a half centuries. The Israelites then became dispersed as minorities, first in Palestine and later further afield. A small number of Jews continued to live in Jerusalem, and some returned from exile to try to rebuild their temple, which had been demolished, and to re-establish the worship of Yahweh.

Throughout the period of the Israelite kingdom, the population of Jerusalem and of Palestine contained a large element of the original Canaanites, who were, as we have seen, of Arab stock.[3] Throughout the early centuries of the Christian era, and after the Islamic conquests of the seventh century AD, Arabs from the Peninsula continued to settle in Palestine in increasing numbers, thus further strengthening the ethnic relationship between the Muslim Arabs of the Peninsula and the inhabitants of the Fertile Crescent who were descended from the earlier pagan Arabs.

The Arab Peninsula, the Fertile Crescent, and Palestine
In ancient times, the term "Arabian Peninsula" covered, in addition to the Peninsula itself, the areas now known as Iraq, Syria, Lebanon, Jordan (earlier Transjordan), and Palestine. It also included Sinai, and even Egypt east of the Nile; the Nile was considered to be the western border of the whole region.

With this connotation, the term "Arabian Peninsula" was in general use from the beginning of the first millennium BC[4]. The expression "Arab countries" was also used. The present use of the term "Arabian Peninsula", referring only to the great peninsula, the northern deserts and Kuwait, is, like many other delineations, a result of the drawing of new political boundaries after the First World War. "The Fertile Crescent" is a term coined by Breasted, the well-known American historian, who used it to describe the area extending from the northern tip of the Arabian Gulf westwards to the fertile lands of the Lower Nile. In more general usage, however, the term nowadays refers only to Iraq, Syria, Lebanon, Palestine and Jordan.

These geographical terms have an important historical significance, for they indicate how these regions provided the sources of livelihood for the peoples and the tribes who inhabited them. It is now firmly established that the heart of the Arabian Peninsula was the place of origin of the peoples who migrated to the Fertile Crescent. It is equally certain that the inhabitants of the Crescent moved freely, regularly and extensively from one part of the territory to another, normally unhindered by any tribal or political boundaries. Since the peoples were in the early days mostly nomadic, the whole area of Peninsula and Crescent combined was regarded as a general homeland, and the various tribes, though dissimilar in some respects, came from a single ethnic stock. There "was no serious language barrier anywhere in the Fertile Crescent,"[5] nor indeed between the Crescent and the Peninsula. The heart of the Peninsula was the cradle of the peoples of Arab origin, and the Fertile Crescent was the nursery of their development and their civilisation. So far as we know, no reverse migrations towards Arabia ever took place. Thus, the people of Arabia have retained their original ethnic and cultural identity throughout recorded time.

The Fertile Crescent

From ancient times, this has been an inseparable part of the Arabian Peninsula. The heart of Arabia was the cradle of the Arab race, the Fertile Crescent its area of development.

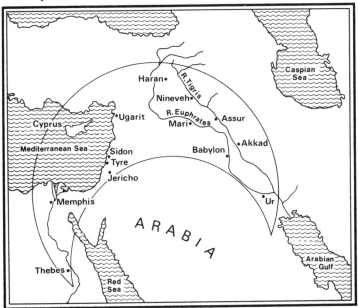

Palestine was named after the Palestinians, or Philistines, who, driven from Crete and other Aegean islands about 1200 BC, settled along the stretch of the Mediterranean coast which extends roughly from Jaffa to Gaza, and which was then part of the land of the Canaanites. The area they occupied and called Philistia extended inland from the coast to the foot of the chain of mountains among which Jerusalem stands; this coastal region lay astride one of the most important routes between Egypt and Syria. After an eventful period lasting nearly a hundred and fifty years, the Philistines were assimilated by the original Amorites and Canaanites. Their invasion from the Mediterranean on the west had almost coincided with the Israelite invasion from the Jordan on the east, which apparently took place in about 1260 BC. The name "Palestine", however, became the name of almost the whole area to which the word refers today and which constituted a major part of the land of the Canaanites, the biblical Canaan. It is not clear why the name persisted and indeed prevailed even after the people themselves ceased to exist as a separate ethnic group.

Semites, Arabs, and their migrations

In the present state of historical terminology, the term "Semite" is vague and often utterly misleading. The word frequently appears in foreign texts to refer to the ancient native peoples of Jerusalem, Palestine, Arabia, or indeed of the countries of the Middle East as a whole. As generally used, it includes the Babylonians, Assyrians, Chaldeans, Amorites, Canaanites and Aramaeans. The term "Semitic" referred originally to languages and cultures, rather than to races or peoples.

While we still use the historical names of such tribes as the Babylonians and the Jebusites, in the modern sense these peoples are all of one ethnic stock: the Arab race, which originated and developed in the heart of Arabia.[6] So, if we are to apply the term "Semite" to a people, it must be to the whole Arab race; the mythological derivation of the word from Shem, the son of Noah, is now generally discredited. However, it is common knowledge that the words "Semite" and "Semitic" are often used to refer specifically and exclusively to the Israelites, and the confusion is compounded by the fact that Hebrew, the language of the Israelites, is one of the Semitic family of languages, as is Arabic also, so

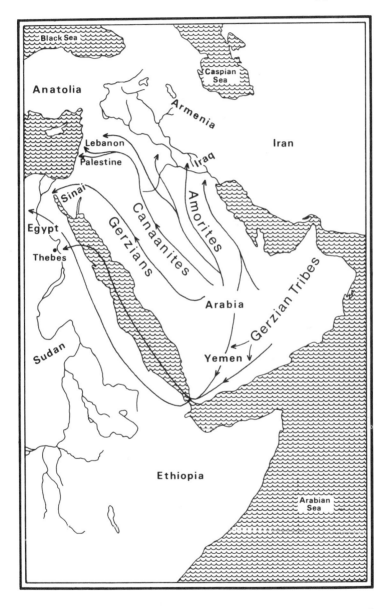

that the terms are often used in a third sense to refer both to the people of the Arab race in general and to the Israelite sub-group in particular. This implies, of course, that the two are of the same race, though recent studies strongly suggest the probability that the Israelites had an altogether different racial origin. We shall return to this point later.

Modern studies of pre-history also indicate that south-west Asia, southern Arabia and Palestine may have been among the places of origin of the earliest fully mature examples of *homo sapiens*, who appeared perhaps forty thousand years ago, having already developed the erect stature, the large cranium and high forehead, the present proportions of the limbs, and above all the high intelligence, which enabled man to move towards the establishment of civilisation.[7]

In that early but protracted stage when all men were nomads, fertile soil was scarce in the Arabian Peninsula, and increases in the population either of men or of domestic animals forced regular migrations—the strongly marked, almost cyclical movements of peoples towards Egypt and the Fertile Crescent. Men moved overland to the southernmost parts of Arabia—Yemen and the Hadramaut—while the Red Sea proved to be no formidable barrier to Egypt. From all over the Peninsula they made their way to Mesopotamia, Syria, Lebanon, Jordan and Palestine, and thence to Egypt across the Sinai desert. Along these same routes, other Arabian tribes moved to Egypt; the Babylonians, Assyrians, Chaldeans, and some of the Amorites moved in successive waves to Syria, Jordan and Palestine; the Canaanites to Syria, Lebanon, and Palestine; the Aramaeans to Syria alone.

The Amorite and Canaanite migrations to Palestine are of special interest to us. The Jebusites, apparently a small tribe of Canaanite stock, seem to have moved into the land where, several centuries later, Jerusalem was built. It was they who initiated the building of what was to become the Holy City. Though archaeology has not yet discovered any evidence of the town's existence before about 2600 BC, its origins may lie in the third or even the fourth millennium. It was the Jebusites, too, it seems, who first conferred on the city its peculiar aura of sanctity.

We cannot here describe in detail the pattern of these early waves of migration. Generally, a single wave would last for a century or two, while the period between two waves was roughly a millennium. They started in about 4500 BC or perhaps even earlier, and were followed by similar waves in about 3500, 2500, and 1500. Other waves occurred at even later dates.

The Islamic conquests which began in about AD 630 may be regarded as another wave of Arab migration, under the banner of Islam. This time, the regions covered were much larger, including not only all the countries of the Fertile Crescent but also Egypt, Sudan, North Africa, Spain, Turkey, Iran and even further afield in the East.[8]

NOTES

1 John Bright, *History of Israel*, 1967, p. 125 (for further details, see Bibliography).
2 Noth, *The History of Israel*, p. 53.
3 The term "Arabs" was, during the first millennium BC, applied as a general ethnic denomination to the various tribes which inhabited Arabia. Earlier designations referred to tribes or places. For simplicity, we use the term "Arabs" for the earlier peoples of the Arab lands.
4 Zeidan, *The Arabs before Islam*, p. 29.
5 Albright, *The Archaeology of Palestine*, p. 204.
6 Hitti, *History of the Arabs*, p. 9.
7 Sonia Cole, *Races of Man* (British Museum), 1965, pp. 44, 46.
8 For detailed discussion of the waves of Arab migration, see Hitti, *History of the Arabs*, p. 11, and Hugo Winkler, *The History of Babylonia and Assyria*, tr. James A. Craig, New York, 1907, pp. 18–22, cited by Hitti.

Chapter Two

Modern Jerusalem

Jerusalem is situated on latitude 32° North, longitude 35° East, about fifty-five kilometres east of the Mediterranean coast, thirty kilometres west of the River Jordan, and twenty-five kilometres south-west of Jericho.

The city stands on a plateau, surrounded by hills, eight hundred metres above sea level. The mean minimum temperature is 10°C, and the mean maximum 35°C. The atmosphere is fairly dry, and the humidity is never high. The mean annual rainfall is about 600 mm.; when it is evenly distributed throughout the winter season, it suffices for the cultivation of grain, vegetables and fruit. The winter season lasts from November to the end of March.

The city is surrounded by some famous mountain peaks: Jabal Masharef (Mount Scopus) to the north, Mukabbir to the south, Zeitun (the Mount of Olives) to the east, and Sahyoun (Mount Zion) to the west. The old city is completely encircled by a wall, four kilometres long and twelve metres high. Seven great gates are set in the wall. The best-known of these are the Damascus Gate in the north, the Dung Gate (Magharba) in the south, St Stephen's Gate in the east and the Jaffa Gate in the west. There is an eighth gate (the Golden) in the east, but this is now walled up. Most of the present wall was erected by the Ottoman Sultan Sulieman the Magnificent; construction started in AD 1563 and went on for five years. Succeeding rulers kept the wall in repair. The old and the modern city together occupy thirty-one square kilometres, or 3,100 hectares. The old city alone occupies only 92.7 hectares.

This purely physical description of Jerusalem can convey no idea of the beauty and the serenity of the city. These can be appreciated only by going there, and the longer one's stay the more strongly does one feel its character and its charm. Its situation is impressive. The air is clear and pure. The slopes of the hills are often covered with Mediterranean shrubs and, in season, with bright and colourful flowers. In the centre, below the surrounding hills, lies Jerusalem itself, distinguished by its many ancient and beautiful buildings.

The material used in both ancient and modern buildings is the local limestone, an attractive stone in various shades of rose. It is very hard and is impervious to water and to humidity, so that no appreciable change in its colour or shade takes place even over relatively long periods. "The stones . . . speak of history long and varied." The deliberate (until recently) avoidance of high buildings has always allowed a view of wide horizons, with alternate bands of lush and arid colours. The Arab inhabitants seem to have been affected by the serenity of their surroundings; their behaviour is civilised yet simple, bred of freedom and of tranquillity. The sanctity of this ancient, Oriental, Arab city gives dignity and depth to the character of its citizens.

Jewish property in Jerusalem

Of the old city, Jews own only 4%, 4 hectares. This area comprises all the Jewish property within the old city. Of the Jewish Quarter itself, which occupies about 3 hectares, Jews, oddly enough, own only 15%; the rest is Muslim property: it belongs to the Muslim religious trusts known as "waqfs".

Of the total area of modern Jerusalem, 3,000 hectares, until 1948 Jews owned only 500 hectares (17%) while Arabs owned the remaining 83%. This fact utterly contradicts the propaganda of the Zionists, who claim that Jerusalem is Jewish.

Jewish-owned property can be listed as follows:

Old Jerusalem:	4% of 93 hectares
Jewish Quarter:	15% of 3 hectares
Modern Jerusalem:	17% of 3,000 hectares

9

The old city, still lying within its ancient walls, has remained completely Arab except for the relatively few Jews in the Jewish Quarter and similar numbers of Armenians and Greeks. Some of the early inhabitants and later immigrants, of whom a number were Jewish, began building outside the walls, but their numbers remained limited and did not change the ratios of population or of ownership. This was the situation before the annexations and changes announced by the Israelis after 1967, which of course rest on no legal or moral basis. The new Arab quarters outside the city walls comprise Sheikh Jarrah, Bab-Essahra, Musrarah, and Lifta to the north and the north-west; Baqa' and Thori to the south; Talbiah, Mamilla, and Qatamon to the west; Ras El-Amoud and Wadi El-Joz to the east.

The sacred and historical monuments of the Holy City are of course of supreme importance. The most famous, perhaps, is the Haram Esh-Sharif, which encloses the Aqsa Mosque and the Mosque of Omar. The main building is known as the Dome of the Rock and is one of the most beautiful edifices in the world. The Haram lies south-east of the centre of the old city, still within the old walls, which encompass some thirty-five other mosques, many cemeteries and religious sites of special significance in Islamic history.

Among the great Christian monuments are the Church of the Holy Sepulchre, in the centre of the old city, the well-known Via Dolorosa, the Church of All Nations on the Mount of Olives, the Gethsemane Church, and other churches and cemeteries of various Christian denominations.

Despite Israeli propaganda, there are in fact no important Jewish monuments or religious sanctuaries in Jerusalem. It is true that there is a Jewish ritual of mourning at the Wailing Wall, but this in fact is a portion of the wall of the Haram Esh-Sharif, and is actually Muslim property. The Israelis assert that the wall is a remnant of Solomon's Temple, but it is in fact part of the outer wall of Herod's Temple. It is historically established that Solomon's Temple has been completely demolished more than once. Archaeological excavations during the last hundred years have yielded no evidence of any part of Solomon's Temple.

There are a number of synagogues and religious buildings in the Jewish Quarter of the old city, but all are of recent construction or usage. None of the synagogues dates back further than the eighteenth century, and most of them are single rooms in Arab-owned or Islamic *waqf* houses, rented to the Jews at nominal rates. There are also a few Jewish cemeteries in Jerusalem, some of which are established on rented Islamic land.

In 1948, the population of Jerusalem was about 160,000, half of them Arabs, half Jews. The large proportion of Jews was due to the implementation of the policy of the Balfour Declaration. In AD 1170, there seems to have been one single Jew living in the city.[1]

Jerusalem is a tourist attraction of world-wide importance, and the income from tourism in 1966 was over twelve million pounds. Tourism is still in the early stages of its development and has, of course, shown enormous possibilities. Jerusalem's attraction has a direct effect on the neighbouring Arab countries, including Egypt and Lebanon. Tourism to Jerusalem might well produce an annual revenue of more than a hundred million pounds.

The association of the name "Israel" with Jerusalem, the most famous city in the world and the venerated centre of three great religions, is of great value to Zionist propaganda. Even more important to the Zionists is the creation of a "unified Jerusalem" under Israeli sovereignty, thrusting deep into the Kingdom of Jordan and well placed to give access to Jordan and the other Arab countries.

Jerusalem has only a few light industries, mainly connected with tourism, and including carving in olive-wood and the manufacture of wax candles, knitted goods, glass and silverware.

Education is widespread and of a quite high standard. The city contains about fifty Arab schools and nearly thirty libraries, some of which are of particular historical value, such as the Khalidiah, the Arab College, St Saviour, Al-Aqsa, the Palestine Museum, and the Dominican, British and American archaeological libraries.

After the war of June 1967, the Zionists proclaimed the annexation of Old Jerusalem to add to the sectors of the city which they had occupied from 1948. In spite of resolutions of the United Nations Security Council, Israel has persisted in its arbitrary measures and has lost no time in converting the city to its own purposes, bulldozing Arab houses, driving out their owners and rendering them homeless, expropriating Arab land and erecting tall new skyscrapers, "match-boxes six storeys high", thus disfiguring the Holy City and destroying its unique character.

The Zionist plan for "greater Jerusalem" aims at the speedy

creation of a *fait accompli* by enlarging the boundaries of the city, settling Jewish immigrants and redesigning the Jewish Quarter. It provides not only for the discordant new buildings but also for night-clubs, bars and small apartments. If it is achieved, the plan will make the Holy City look like a vast petrol station. Towards the end of 1970, the plan was presented to a conference in Israel of thirty civil engineers, architects and artists from all over the world. The plan has foundered under the weight of criticism heaped upon it by the expert advisers; the reason, in the advisers' view, was its violation of "the special character and atmosphere of Jerusalem." Professor Bronsvy, a Jewish participant in the conference, has stated that the proposed constructions are an act of mass suicide, committed as a result of utter failure. Addressing Teddy Kollek, the mayor, he said that if Kollek attempted to secure approval of the plan Bronsvy would have to declare that it was a very bad one, and that the engineers would not watch in silence what Kollek, without any proper mandate, was doing to the city. According to Bronsvy, the plan constituted a potent weapon in the hands of the Arabs.

Bronsvy's phrase "what Kollek was doing to the city" referred to the enormous apartment buildings erected north of Jerusalem in what was called the Eshkol Quarter, and to similar structures that violated the character of the city and can be rendered tolerable only by demolition.

Apart from the illegality of the Israeli actions, the development of the city should clearly be left to its rightful inhabitants. Neither now nor in the past have the Israelis shown any appreciation of the cultural heritage of Palestine. They have not had either the time or the inclination to absorb the spirit of that heritage. The Arabs, who have owned the land from time immemorial and have developed its culture, alone have the rights and the responsibility to develop it, for Arab culture is not only predominant in the area, it is almost the only truly indigenous culture. History creates in a people a sense of history, and this should be the criterion. During the British Mandate, Arab engineers developed the city extensively, yet they preserved and perpetuated the special character and atmosphere of Jerusalem. The same Arab engineers, many of them Egyptians, were able to repair the Aqsa Mosque, the Dome of the Rock and other Muslim and Christian monuments without violating their physical or spiritual character. The heritage and the holiness of the city have not penetrated the hearts or the minds of the Zionists.

Jerome Caminada wrote in *The Times* of 3 March 1971: "If Israel wants to feel the full pulse of the city, once and for all, and relish it in the decades to come, she will hold her hand now." Caminada goes on to emphasise that the old city should be returned to its aboriginal inhabitants: the Palestinians.

NOTE

1 Fr Eugene Hoade, *Guide to the Holy Land*, p. 71.

Chapter Three

The Emergence of Ancient Jerusalem and its Arab Inhabitants

Jerusalem was by far the most famous city of the ancient East. On the mosaic map in the floor of the sixth century church at Madaba in Jordan, and on other early Christian maps, Jerusalem is shown as the centre of the world. Its fame persists today.

Archaeological research in and around Jerusalem has revealed human settlement dating back over forty thousand years to the Neolithic, Mesolithic and Palaeolithic ages,[1] and in the opinion of some scholars the Arab race may have existed in this area as long as ten thousand years or more ago.

W. F. Albright, the American archaeologist and linguist, has said: "The dominant bony structure and skull-form of the purest known Hamitic and Semitic tribes until today already appear in the Mesolithic of Palestine, nearly 10,000 years ago. Without denying that there were many movements of non-Semitic peoples across Palestinian soil between that date and the third millennium BC, it seems only reasonable to suppose that the Semitic element has remained primary in the ethnic make-up of Palestine ever since."[2]

As we have seen, it is now well established that the Arabian Peninsula and the Fertile Crescent were, to the Arabs, one unified area, and that its peoples came from the heart of Arabia. There is no doubt that major migrations took place between 5000 and 3000 BC, nor that at some time between 4000 and 3000 BC these peoples began the occupation of the present area of Jerusalem. This is attested by the discovery in caves of flint arrowheads, scrapers, and kitchen pots. Ap-Thomas, Senior Lecturer at the University College of Bangor in Wales, says: "Long before history proper begins, there were men in and around Jerusalem ... The Amorites were a nomadic Semitic people who apparently settled down in Palestine to found the prosperous towns of the Middle Bronze Age."[3] This must have been some two or three thousand years before the arrival of the Hebrews in Jerusalem.

Although some scholars have regarded Jerusalem as an Amorite foundation, it seems more likely to have been Jebusite, as we saw in our first chapter. In the opinion of Dame Kathleen Kenyon, the celebrated archaeologist, the Amorites arrived in about 2300 BC, but "there was probably occupation at Jerusalem about 2600 BC, in the early Bronze Ages, when the occupants of Palestine were certainly Semitic, i.e. of ancient Arab stock, and some authorities believe they were Canaanites ... The earliest fortified town of Jerusalem of which there is certain evidence was founded about 1800 BC."[4] This would be about 800 years before the Hebrews reached Jerusalem. Remains of those periods surviving at Jerusalem have been found, but so far these are few.

The ancient city stands on the Ophel ridge. The reason for the selection of the site must have been both strategic and religious. The ridge overlooks deep valleys on every side except the north, where it is linked with the Moriah. It lies near the main route between Palestine and Egypt, and near the cross-roads of the routes from Nablus to Hebron and from Jericho to the Mediterranean. It was on the Ophel ridge that the oldest known inhabitants built their *heikal* (temple) to their "Most High God", Salem. The king of Jerusalem was then also "the priest of the Most High God".

The proximity of the spring Jihon, in the valley east of the ridge, must have been decisive in the choice of the site; for Zion, to the west, is higher and larger than Ophel, but further from the spring.[5] Ophel is about 400 metres from north to south and 135 metres from east to west. The area of ancient Jerusalem was about 4.7 hectares.

This was the place where, so far as we know, the Arab Jebusites founded their city. According to both Arab and western authorities, they gave it the names of Jebus, after their own tribe, and Salem (in Arabic: safe) after one of their earlier chiefs. Thus, the Israelites had nothing to do with the founding of the city nor with its peculiar sanctity; both were present centuries before their arrival.

Ancient Jerusalem was built up gradually. Some of the Jebusite

15

tribes lived around the Ophel ridge in the neighbouring plains and valleys. They occupied caves, tents of goat-hair, or simple mud or stone houses forming villages clustered around the ridge. Breasted says: "Standing on the hills one could see the village houses and their shepherd owners, with their herds, grazing over the hills, coming under the observer's eyes."[6]

Ophel declines to the east to the foot of the Kedron valley. Ancient Jerusalem was extended towards the east and so supporting walls were necessary against which the ground could be levelled and houses built. Archaeological evidence shows that heavy rains or earth tremors caused the collapse of these walls.

During the second millennium BC the built-up area of Jerusalem was about 3.4 hectares, so Ophel was not entirely covered with buildings. We have no certain figure for the number of inhabitants at the time, but to judge from the congestion of the houses and the narrowness of the streets it could not have exceeded three thousand. The built-up area was extended as time went by, but was limited by the presence of the valleys. Parts, but not all, of the Jebusite wall have been excavated; it bears no relation to the present wall of the old city.

To provide access to the Jihon spring in the valley, the inhabitants carved a tunnel through the rocks; this was especially important in time of siege. It seems that when David's initial attack had been unable to breach the defences he used this route. The early city seems to have had a northern gate opening on to a road that led to the spring: the modern road is superimposed on this, or perhaps lies parallel to it. The other source of water was Bir Ayoub, the Well of Job, which lies 200 metres south of Ophel and was thus useless during sieges.

In time, the settlement grew large enough to be regarded as one of the city-states the form of which the Canaanites had copied from Mesopotamia and had developed in Palestine. Life in the area had followed first the nomadic, bedouin pattern and had then evolved into village communities. A city-state, however, comprised a number of tribes or sub-tribes, with the more affluent families living in the city and the rest around it. Bedouin life depended upon the grazing of herds, village life on agriculture; towns and cities lived primarily on trade and handicrafts, and the social structure was semi-feudal. The system of city-states had its advantages, but it led to disunity and weakness in the political life of the

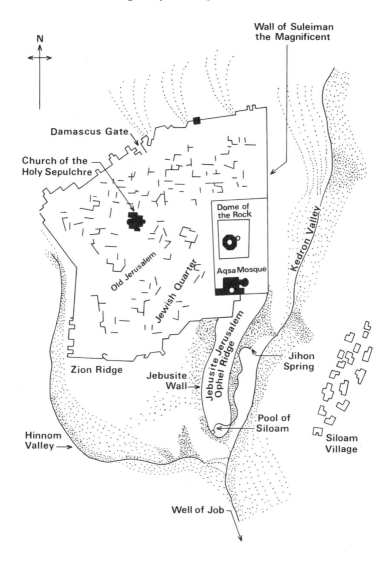

Jebusite and Ancient Jerusalem
This shows the site of the original Jebusite foundation, the probable point of entry by David at Jihon Spring, and the later development within the wall.

The Beni-Hassan Tablet
The tablet depicts Amorites trading between the land of Cannan and Egypt.

Canaanites. The various cities did not unite to form large kingdoms, and their enemies thus found them relatively easy prey. Hence it was not possible for the Canaanites to develop a culture of the kind that came into existence in the Nile valley and in Mesopotamia.

Archaeology does not and probably never will provide a list of the Jebusite kings of Jerusalem. We have to rely largely on the Old Testament, which gives the names of Salem, Melchizedek, Adoni Zedek, and Adoni Bezek. It also suggests that at the time of Abraham's supposed passage through the city, which appears to have taken place in about 1900 BC, Jebus must already have been a complete city, with a commanding site, temples of worship, and an aura of special sanctity. Canaanite and Jebusite towns had by then reached a relatively high level of culture and civilisation, long before the first appearance of the Israelites about 900 years later.

NOTES

1 *Encyclopaedia Britannica*, 1963, article on Jerusalem.
2 Albright, *The Archaeology of Palestine*, pp. 179–80.
3 Ap-Thomas, article in *Archaeology and Old Testament Study*, p. 82.
  See also Lionel Cust, *Jerusalem* (A. & C. Black), London 1924, p. 19.
  Some authorities think that the Amorites founded no towns.
4 From notes by Dr Kathleen Kenyon.
5 "Zion" is a Canaanite word meaning "hill". It is odd that a proto-Arabic
  word is used to denote a movement which ignores the Canaanites and
  fights against their race. See *Encyclopaedia Britannica*, 1963, article on
  Zion.
6 Albright, op. cit., p. 155 (retranslation from the Arabic translation).

Chapter Four

The Sanctity of Jerusalem and its Arabic Names

Recent archaeological excavations in Jebusite Jerusalem have indicated the existence of characteristic pagan temples closely resembling Canaanite temples erected to their most popular god, Ba'al, and to other deities. In Jerusalem, the Jebusites had a special temple erected to their supreme god, Salem, which was constructed on Mount Ophel; hence their designation of the city as holy and its name "the city of the god Salem".

When, according to the Old Testament, Abraham passed through Jerusalem in about 1900 BC, the city had been a holy place for an appreciable time. We are told that the Patriarch received a blessing from Melchizedek (Arabic: "the truthful king") King of Salem, "priest of the Most High God". He blessed Abraham in these words: "Blessed be Abraham by the Most High God, possessor of heaven and earth." This blessing indicates a developed stage of religious belief. Abraham paid the Jebusite king "tithes of all his possessions" (*Genesis*, 14: 18–20). It is evident that Melchizedek combined the roles of priest and king, as did most of the Canaanite kings of the time. It is worth considering the length of time needed for a simple pagan religion to attain, in those days, such a relatively advanced stage of development.

The Israelites were also, on their arrival much later, to regard Jerusalem as a sacred city. In tracing the evolution of their religious beliefs, one can see that they started by following Jebusite and Canaanite forms of ritual. Even after their own religion was developed and Yahweh adopted as their unique and special god, there were whole periods as well as isolated cases of Israelite reversion to the worship of Ba'al and other Jebusite and Canaanite gods (*Jeremiah* 32: 35). Even the followers of Moses, who preached monotheism, showed similar religious instability. King Solomon's famous temple was built on Jebusite and Canaanite models; this is quite understandable in the case of a nomadic tribe, as the Israelites then were, with a precarious new identity and at an early stage of religious and cultural development. Modern Zionist propaganda, however, ignores the facts and evades the truth, and by its sheer weight and intensity convinces many people that Jerusalem was from its inception a Jewish city and that Palestine and even other Arab territory is the Promised Land and the Land of Israel.

The ancient names given to Jerusalem clearly indicate the Arab origin and character of the city. The Bible mentions Jebus (*Judges* 19: 10–11 and *I Chronicles* 11: 4–5) and records that it belonged to the Jebusites, who for more than two centuries repelled the Israelite invasion. When Jerusalem was conquered, the Jebusites did not leave their city (*Joshua* 15: 63).

Some scholars think that the name Ur-Salem may have preceded the name Jebus. "Uru-Salimmu" is a form found in some cuneiform inscriptions; and "Ur-Salem" was found in the Tel El-Amarna tablets which were sent by Abd-Hiba, the Arab governor of Jerusalem during the fourteenth century BC, and by rulers of other towns, to the Pharaoh of Egypt, whose vassals they were. The tablets contain requests for help against the attacks of the "Habiru" who had by then begun their attempts to conquer Palestine. The form "Ur-Shaleem" appears in Egyptian texts of the nineteenth and eighteenth centuries BC; that is, at about the time of Abraham's visit. In the Assyrian archives of Sennacherib, dated from the seventh century BC, appears the form "Uri-Salimmu". The form of the name as it is now used by the Israelis is "Yeru-Shala'im", which derives from the usage of the Arab Aramaeans, who migrated from Arabia to Syria. The Hebrew language, as we have seen, derives directly from the Canaanite and Aramaean tongues.[1]

When David took Jerusalem, he called it the "City of David", and the name Jebus began to disappear. But the king's personal name for the city did not endure for long, and the name Ur-Shalem returned to general use. The name "Bezek", which also appears in the Bible (*Judges* 1: 4–5), is thought by some scholars to be another

21

name for Jerusalem, deriving from the Jebusite king Adoni Bezek, the successor to Adoni Zedek, who was king at the time of Joshua's attack on the city.

At the beginning of the second century AD, Hadrian, the Roman Emperor who conquered the city, gave it the name Aelia Capitolina, from his family name Aelius; this name, together with Ur-Shaleem, was used from the middle of the fourth century AD. When Omar, the second Muslim Caliph, entered the city in AD 638, he wrote the name Aelia in his covenant with the Christian—mostly Arab—inhabitants.

After the Muslim conquest, several modern Arabic names appeared. Among them were Al-Quds, Beit El-Maqdes, and Dar-es-Salaam. In proto-Arabic (proto-Semitic) "Al-Quds" means "pure" or "sacred"; it also means "high cultivable land". "Beit El-Maqdes" means "house of purity"—where abominations are washed away; this is the meaning of the phrase in the Koran. "Dar-es-Salaam" and similar names are synonyms of Ur-Salem, for Salaam is a variant of Salem.

Thus, all the historical names of Jerusalem are of Arabic origin, ancient or modern, with the exception of the personal names conferred by the temporary conquerors David and Hadrian, and neither of those names lasted long. The Jews may be able to claim one version of the name of the city: Yar'a Shalm. According to their tradition, Shem, son of Noah, called it "Shalm": peace. Abraham called it "Yar'a": fear. God then merged the two names: Yar'a Shalm, or Ur-Shaleem. This is clearly legend and not history.

NOTE

1 Hitti, *History of Syria*, p. 164.

Chapter Five

Early Jerusalem: Language and Culture

If, as has been suggested, *homo sapiens* developed first in Arabia and Palestine, as well as in East Africa and West Asia, one of the main reasons would have been the favourable climate and the resultant fertility of the land.[1] The subsequent advance of human culture was more rapid as experience accumulated and as each new discovery and invention opened fresh potentialities.

When the Amorite, Canaanite, Jebusite and Phoenician tribes originally left the heart of Arabia, migrating to Palestine and other parts of the Fertile Crescent, they had already achieved a relatively high degree of ability and imagination. This enabled them to exploit their new habitat with improved agricultural methods, to establish villages and towns, to move towards higher stages of culture, and to take what some consider to be the decisive step towards civilisation: the invention of writing. Writing, which enabled man to record past experience, was one of the crucial factors in his development.

Between the fourth and third millennia BC, much of this progress had already been made. An important social innovation was the system of city-states, which appeared throughout the area and was later to be adopted by the Greeks. In Mesopotamia and Egypt the great tribes of Arab origin—the Chaldeans, Assyrians, Babylonians, Jerzeans and others—were able to form dynasties and empires. In Palestine such development was checked for geographic reasons, especially lack of water. The city-state system never got beyond the first stage, of cities surrounded by habitations of all kinds and each acting as a fortress within the walls of which all the inhabitants could take refuge in time of attack. The head of the whole community would be a prominent sheikh, as Melk (owner) or King.

Initially, Jerusalem was just such a city-state, with nothing distinguishing it from others, but its central location and its continued sanctity were to give it a unique status. The ethnic stock of its inhabitants was, as we have said, purely Arab: long-headed, fine-featured and of medium stature. During the early millennia after the founding of the city, the Hebrews were unknown, for their identity as "Israel" did not develop until about 1300 BC, when Moses led the exodus from Egypt; or it could be dated from as late as about 1000 BC, when they consolidated their position in Palestine. The weight of scholarly opinion is against regarding Abraham as the forerunner of Israel; the relationship between Abraham and the Israelites is far from certain, and his religion was different from theirs.[2].

The language of the people of Jerusalem was, according to the orientalists' classification, proto-Semitic: proto-Arabic. There are many points of similarity between the Canaanite language and the modern Arabic which developed later. *Beit* (house) in proto-Arabic and modern Arabic is identical to the Canaanite noun; proto-Arabic *ahu* (brother) is *akhu* in both modern Arabic and Canaanite; proto-Arabic and modern Arabic *ein* (eye) is *en* in Canaanite. The evolution of the Canaanite tongue, however, gave rise to a dialect which is not always so easy to compare with the Arabic which emerged in the southern parts of Arabia and which was later to become the dominant Arab dialect.

The scripts show less similarity. Canaanite writing was derived partly from Egyptian hieroglyphics, partly from cuneiform, which was invented in Mesopotamia; in shape the characters are closer to cuneiform. The script is similar to Phoenician and to an ancient Arabic script of southern Arabia, but the simplification which led to Canaanite on the one hand and to linear Arabic on the other produced scripts which are widely dissimilar except in minor respects. The Hebrew script, like the Hebrew language, derives directly from Aramaic.

While archaeology has revealed the writing and thus the language of early Jerusalem, it can tell us nothing of the domestic architecture, for none has survived. On the analogy of contemporary towns such as Jericho and Tel Beit Mersim, and with our knowledge of the stone used, we can nevertheless conjure up a picture of the city in ancient times with some assurance. The houses were built of local materials, mostly hard limestone. Rooms were small, buildings congested, streets narrow and tortuous. Single-storey building was the rule. As time went on, a few two-storey buildings arose, with the ground floor used for storing fodder and other materials. It seems that the flow of water in the rainy season made necessary the construction of channels for sewage. Roofs were made of rubble or mud spread over wooden beams or branches, sealed by an upper layer of limestone mortar. Domed roofs, on the pattern of those in Mesopotamia, were often constructed. Rainwater was drained from the roofs into cisterns in houses or courtyards, for use in the dry season, a system still used in modern Arab villages and small towns.

The principal means of transport until about 1800 BC was the ass; the horse and the camel were domesticated in the region later: the camel in about 1200 BC, the horse a little earlier. The wild camel had, of course, long been known in Arabia; the horse was introduced from central Asia and Asia Minor, and was carefully bred and nurtured to develop and perpetuate the fine qualities of the Arabian horse.

Contemporary carvings and inscriptions depict the clothes of the people. They wore mantles down to the knee, with short trousers underneath. Later, long shirts were worn covering the knees, with or without trousers. Sometimes the mantle, for both men and women, hung from one shoulder only: there was also a skirt-like garment reaching from the waist to below the knee. The longer mantle, girdled at the waist, seems to have arrived later; it is still worn in the countryside by some bedouin but is now rare in the towns.

The clothing is quite well illustrated in the Beni-Hassan tablet, which pictures a small tribe of Palestinian and Jordanian Amorites in 1900 BC. Women's clothes were longer than men's, and the head-dress was normally a shawl wrapped as a turban around the head. In these early days clothing was made from animal skins and furs; woven wool and linen followed later. Shoes were made from skins; sandals for men and high boots for women. Women also wore ornaments such as earrings, pins, beads and shells. Kohl (eye-shadow) was used for protection as well as for adornment.

25

The clothing of the Israelites differed in many respects from that of the Canaanites; it was derived largely from the Hittites of Asia Minor and from the inhabitants of Armenia and neighbouring regions. Albright tells us: "The men of Israel wear long fringed tunics, over which are fringed mantles, both presumably of wool; on their heads they wear short stocking caps, which are bound in place like turbans, while on their feet they wear high boots, turned up at the toes in Hittite fashion." Later, the tunics "were drawn up to the knees and fastened in place by their girdles, while the women are shown with long tunics and mantles."[3]

Archaeological and literary sources indicate a change in clothing and in habits which the Israelites underwent after they invaded Palestine; these show the influence of the Canaanite inhabitants.

As food, the Canaanites consumed wheat, barley and lentils. The stone querns found in excavations show that they knew how to make flour; the modern quern used today by almost every peasant family is a direct development. In Jericho, an oven dating from 1300 BC or even earlier has been excavated; it is very similar to the present Arab village oven, or *taboun*.

In swampy areas, rice was grown. This was used instead of wheat for cooking with lentils; *mujaddara* thus cooked is still a favourite dish in Palestine and neighbouring countries. Milk, *lebban* (similar to yoghourt) and cheese were common. Olives, molasses and vines were known, as were various kinds of meat, especially mutton and various birds. Fish were obtained from Lake Tiberias and from the sea off Jaffa. A staple dish, made of cooked meat with bread, was similar to the modern *mansaf*, which is known in one form or another in nearly every Arab country. Cucumber, onions, garlic and leeks were known from early days: tomatoes, beans, bananas, apricots, peaches and most of the citrus fruits became widely used only in a later age.

NOTES

1 Sonia Cole, *Races of Man*, pp. 44, 46, 50, 59, 61, 63.
2 Dr Susa of Baghdad separates Abraham, as an Amorite or Arab, from any genealogical or religious relationship with the Hebrews. He does the same with Moses. For Dr Susa, Judaism began with the writing of the Bible some 500 years BC, after the exodus to Mesopotamia. (See Dr Susa, *The Arabs and the Jews in History*.) Some western scholars think that the story of Abraham is a myth.
3 Albright, *The Archaeology of Palestine*, p. 212.

Chapter Six

Foreign Invasions of Jerusalem

The first migratory waves from the heart of Arabia to the Fertile Crescent may not have found the area vacant. Remains of human types from well before the tenth century BC have been discovered: Palestine Man, or Carmel Man, seems to have been contemporary with Neanderthal Man of Western Europe; the later Mediterranean Man may have come from the Mediterranean coasts or islands, but is equally likely to have originated in Arabia.[1]

The arrival of the Canaanites by no means marked the final incursion of a whole people into the area. In succeeding ages, migrating peoples came from the north and the east, from Asia Minor, Armenia, the Caucasus, Turkestan and Iran. Seeking fertile land for settlement they crossed the seas, mountains and rivers which separated them from the Crescent. Of particular importance were the Hyksos, the Hittites, the Hurrians and the Philistines. Their invasions all took place between 2000 and 1000 BC. Whatever their influence or effect may have been, they undoubtedly disturbed the quite complex culture of the long-established Canaanites; but in every case the new immigrants were either absorbed and assimilated by the Canaanites or eventually left the country. The inhabitants remained basically Canaanite, Jebusite and Amorite.

The Hyksos are of uncertain origin according to modern scholars, although they were formerly considered to be a Semitic people. They were probably a mixture of Asiatic, Caucasian and Arab tribes. Between about 1700 and 1500 BC they established a sizeable empire which included Jerusalem and its surrounding area. Their dominance, however, did not last more than 150 years, although they remained in the country for much longer. They are mentioned in the Old Testament as one of the peoples who inhabited Jerusalem.

The Hittites came from Asia Minor, where they had established a kingdom which extended from Aleppo to the Black Sea and westward to the site of modern Ankara. This empire flourished between 1750 and 1450 BC. During the fourteenth and thirteenth centuries BC its boundaries were extended, but to the south it did not extend beyond Damascus: it never included Jerusalem. Individual families and small groups of Hittites lived in Palestine, however, especially around Hebron and Ramallah. The Old Testament speaks of them as inhabitants of Palestine and Jerusalem, and tells us that some of Solomon's numerous wives were Hittite. For an appreciable period the Hittite kingdom was contemporaneous with the Hurrian kingdom.

The Hurrians are the Hivites of the Old Testament, which regards them as one of the peoples of Palestine. They originated in Armenia and in the regions around the Black Sea, and they established a kingdom in about 1500 BC. Parts of this lay to the north of the Fertile Crescent, parts within it: it ended in about 1200 BC. Only small groups of Hurrians lived in Palestine, some in the area of Nablus near ancient Samaria, some in the north.

The Philistines, whom we mentioned in our first chapter as having given their name to Palestine, arrived in the land of Canaan after an abortive attempt to enter Egypt from the Mediterranean. They landed between Jaffa and Gaza and were able to establish control over most of the area between the coast and the foot of the Jerusalem mountains. They did not, however, reach the Holy City. Their rule did not last for much longer than 150 years, during which time they were very much under Egyptian influence. As time passed, they adopted not only the religion of the Canaanites but also their language and their way of life, merging eventually with the native population and disappearing as a separate nation.

During the period of their dominance the Philistines clashed with the Hebrews who were coming in from the east. It was during these conflicts that Samson, the strong man and one of the judges of Israel, made his appearance. According to John Bright, "he was an engaging rogue whose fabulous strength and bawdy pranks became legendary."[2] Contrary to later Western legend—such as that popularised by Hollywood—his attacks on the Philistines had disastrous results for the Israelites themselves.

The Israelite invasion, as we have seen, ended miserably after seventy years and many families were exiled to Mesopotamia. Those remaining in Palestine tended to live in seclusion in their own "ghettoes", as did many of those who fled to other countries. That might have been the end of the story as far as Palestine was concerned, but for the Zionist movement which has in recent years led to the mass immigration of Jews into Palestine. Our firm conviction is that this new invasion will also end in the dissolution of the "State" of Israel and the ultimate disappearance of the Zionist ideology.

NOTES

1 Sonia Cole, *Races of Man*, p. 61.
2 John Bright, *History of Israel*, p. 156.

Chapter Seven

The Earliest Jewish Association with Jerusalem

The Jews claim that Abraham was the father of their race.[1] According to the Old Testament, Abraham came to Palestine from Mesopotamia, passing through Syria and arriving in the region of Shechem, near modern Nablus, where Yahweh is said to have promised "this land" to him and to his descendants. The area was not clearly defined, but land to the east and west of Nablus was apparently indicated.

However, it is clear from the Old Testament that Abraham did not take the promise seriously, and did not settle there to take possession of the land. He soon moved on towards Jerusalem and then wandered southwards until he came to Egypt. Later he returned to Palestine, and when his wife Sarah died at Hebron he bought a piece of land there to bury her, but there was never any suggestion in his subsequent actions that he regarded the land as his by virtue of a divine promise. Quite the contrary, for he said to the sons of Heth: "I am a stranger and a sojourner with you: give me possession of a burying place with you . . .", and when they offered him the choice of their sepulchres, "Abraham stood up, and bowed himself to the people of the land," (*Genesis* 23: 4–7). The Bible speaks of him as being a Hebrew, a term we shall be discussing.

Abraham was succeeded by his son Isaac,[2] who was followed in turn by his son Jacob. Both Isaac and Jacob tried to buy land near Nablus, but the inhabitants refused to sell. Yahweh promised to them and to their descendants Palestine and the land from the Nile to the Euphrates. In spite of that divine assurance, Jacob and his children went to Egypt, where their offspring settled and increased in number and mixed with an assortment of outcasts to form a poor, exploited community known there as the Hebrews. They did not feel at home in Egypt, while the Egyptians "might not eat bread with the Hebrews, for that is an abomination unto the Egyptians," (*Genesis* 43: 32). Finally they left Egypt in about 1300 BC, under the leadership of Moses but in disunited and disorganised groups.

According to the Old Testament, after forty years of wandering in the wilderness Moses tried to lead them into Palestine from the south, but they were afraid of the Canaanites and turned to the east bank of the River Jordan. Here the Amorites and the Edomites opposed them near the present town of Kerak, forcing them to change their course towards the Gulf of Aqaba, then to Maan and Madaba. Moses is said to have died here, and his people were then led by Joshua, who invaded Jericho in about 1250 BC.

The "Habiru", the Jewish Invaders of Jerusalem

The origin of the Hebrews is complex and obscure. Many historians identify them with the "Habiru" or "Apiru", of whom Abraham was one, but the Hebrews who entered Palestine do not appear to have been a pure ethnic group. Most scholars describe them as a complex mixture of races, comprising both the heterogeneous group who fled from Egypt and a similar group of unattached wanderers who roamed about in the Fertile Crescent between 2000 and 1000 BC. It was Moses who founded their religion; not, as we have seen, Abraham.

The American historian John Bright, the German Martin Noth, and the British archaeologist Kathleen Kenyon all conclude that the Habiru did not have a single racial origin, because they had no distinguishing names or occupations, some of them being professional mercenaries, others ordinary labourers, and yet others slaves. The one feature that they all had in common was that they were regarded as foreigners. They did not appear to belong to any section of the old-established population, but represented certain restless elements who had "no roots in the soil". As mercenaries they were recruited from nomadic groups or marauding bands of adventurers in search of rich lands to invade. They may have consisted of Hittites, Hurrians and Asians from beyond the rivers and mountains bordering the Fertile Crescent, and they were joined by nomads and outcasts from the Arabian Peninsula and from the Fertile Crescent itself.

The warriors who gathered round David seem to have had similarly diverse origins: "David therefore departed thence. And every one that was in distress and every one that was in debt, and every one that was discontented gathered themselves unto him, and he became a captain over them, and there were with him about four hundred men," (*I Samuel* 22: 1, 2). John Bright, though sympathetic towards the Jews, does not hesitate to say that "for some time David pursued a precarious existence as a bandit chief (a Khapiru)."[3]

It appears then that the Hebrews, a nomadic people of mixed and uncertain origin, devoted their energies to mercenary service and invaded the Canaanite city-states of Palestine, spreading devastation and terror, ousting the original inhabitants and seizing their land and their property. This is the story that emerges from the Old Testament; it forms part of the Jewish heritage and recurs in modern times in the precepts and practice of Zionism in Palestine.

Because of their lack of obvious origins, the Hebrews chose to regard Abraham, who was himself supposed to be a Habiru, as the founder of their "race". They were divided into twelve tribes. They claimed that their God, Yahweh, promised the land of Palestine to them, a claim made explicitly in the Old Testament. This is not the place to speculate on the justice or injustice of such a claim; suffice it to say that Yahweh was the tribal God of the Hebrews and that they were his chosen race.

A close observer can hardly resist the temptation to regard Zionist Israel of today as a Habiru state. The foreign origins, the mixture of races, the "professional" wars of aggression and expansion, the brutalities and the injustice are common to both situations, the ancient and the modern. Indeed, some Zionist leaders, such as Eleazer Livneh, have spoken of modern Israelis living in an age similar to that of Joshua. The Arabs can hardly be blamed for agreeing with this view.

Not only were the Hebrews regarded as foreigners by the original inhabitants of Palestine; they looked upon themselves as strangers there. During the period after they had entered the

33

country under the leadership of Joshua but before their capture of Jerusalem, an Israelite couple and their servant once found themselves benighted. "And when they were by Jebus, the day was far spent, and the servant said unto his master, Come, I pray thee, and let us turn into this city of the Jebusites, and lodge in it. And his master said unto him, We will not turn aside hither into the city of a stranger, that is not of the children of Israel," (*Judges* 19: 11–12). At that time, Jerusalem was some three thousand years old, and Arab tribes had inhabited the area for all that time and a thousand years more.

In 1260 BC, Jerusalem was under the Egyptian sphere of influence. Even earlier than this, its governor Abd-Hiba had appealed to the Pharaoh for help. "Let the king turn his attention to the archers, and let the king, my lord, send out fifty-five troops of archers, for the king has no lands left. The Apiru plunder all the lands of the king. If there are archers here in this year the lands of the king will remain intact."[4] But the Pharaoh was otherwise occupied and failed to come to the governor's rescue. F. F. Bruce quotes the following message: "If only the king would send fifty soldiers the situation around Jerusalem could be restored."[5] The Old Testament states that Joshua besieged Jericho, razed the city walls, burnt the houses, and slaughtered all the men, women and children, as Moses had commanded before his death and as Yahweh had ordered.

Joshua's army was small, and consisted of men who had infiltrated into the country over a long period. Dr Kenyon says: "The archaeological record does not provide the evidence of a large-scale incursion, contemporary with the destruction of Jericho . . . The entry was not in great force but was rather that of a small band which gradually established itself in the country, and gradually brought under its influence the allied tribes, the other Habiru."[6] The Old Testament mentions the resistance to the invasion of Jericho put up by the inhabitants of the area, the Amorites, Canaanites, Hittites, Girgashites, Hivites and Jebusites.

From Jericho, the invaders advanced as far as Ai, near modern Ramallah; they destroyed it and marched on to Jerusalem. The inhabitants of the city fought bravely and repelled them, and Joshua died before he could enter it. The resistance is thus described by Breasted: "On entering Palestine the Hebrews found the Canaanites already dwelling there in flourishing towns

The Inhabitants of Palestine, before 1260 BC
This shows the city-states of the Arab peoples.

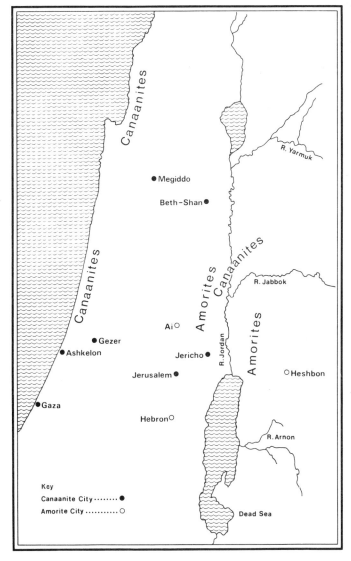

Canaanites

R. Yarmuk

● Megiddo

Beth-Shan ●

Canaanites

Amorites   Canaanites

R. Jabbok

Canaanites

Ai ○

Amorites

● Gezer

● Ashkelon

Jericho ●

R. Jordan

Amorites

Jerusalem ●

○ Heshbon

● Gaza

Hebron ○

R. Arnon

Key
Canaanite City ········ ●
Amorite City ··········· ○

Dead Sea

protected by massive walls. The Hebrews were able to capture only the weaker Canaanite towns. As the rough Hebrew shepherds looked across the highlands of North Palestine they beheld their kindred scattered over far-stretching hilltops, with the frowning walls of many a Canaanite stronghold rising between them. Even Jerusalem in the Judaean highlands for centuries defied the Hebrew invaders."

Breasted also says: "Let us remember that these unconquered Canaanite towns now possessed a civilisation fifteen hundred years old, with comfortable houses, government, industries, trade, writing and religion—a civilisation which the rude Hebrew shepherds were soon adopting; for they could not avoid intercourse with the unsubdued Canaanite towns, as trade and business threw them together. This mingling with the Canaanites produced the most profound changes in the life of the Hebrews. Most of them left their tents and began to build houses like those of the Canaanites; they put off the rough sheepskin they had worn in the desert, and they put on fine Canaanite raiment of gaily-coloured woven wool. After a time, in appearance, occupation and manner of life the Hebrews were not to be distinguished from the Canaanites among whom they now lived. In short, they had adopted Canaanite civilisation, just as newly-arrived immigrants among us soon adopt our clothing and our ways."[7]

According to the Old Testament, "The children of Benjamin did not drive out the Jebusites that inhabited Jerusalem; but the Jebusites dwell with the children of Benjamin in Jerusalem to this day," (*Judges* 1: 21). But the Jebusites were not alone in resisting the Hebrew invaders in Jerusalem and the surrounding area. The Canaanites, the Philistines and others opposed the invasion and continued to inhabit the various parts of Palestine.

Having failed to conquer Jerusalem, Joshua attacked the less protected villages and captured them despite resistance. The main reasons for his success were the disunity of the city-states, the weakening rule of Egypt and its failure to send aid, and the professional skill of his soldiers with their violent greed for land and wealth. The Book of Joshua gives details of the lands conquered and distributed among the leader's followers. The invaders were few in number, however, and the land taken was limited; at one stage the verdict is: "There remaineth yet very much land to be possessed," (*Joshua* 13: 1). Some authorities say that this distribution of land did not in fact take place then but that the account reflects a much later situation.

Throughout their history, the Israelites continued the practices of the invaders under Joshua: plunder, slaughter and eviction of the original inhabitants. These practices were later sanctified by their religion, for Yahweh addresses his people in these terms: "And it shall be, when the Lord thy God shall have brought thee into the land which he sware unto thy fathers, to Abraham, to Isaac, and to Jacob, to give thee great and goodly cities, which thou buildedst not, and houses full of good things, which thou filledst not, and wells digged which thou diggedst not, vineyards and olive trees, which thou plantedst not, when thou shalt eat and be full . . ." (*Deuteronomy* 6: 10–11).

And again: "The Lord thy God will put out those nations before thee by little and little: thou mayest not consume them at once, lest the beasts of the field increase upon thee."

The Jewish Conquest of Jerusalem

Joshua was succeeded by those rulers of the Israelites whose names are recorded in the Book of Judges; then came Saul and David, who were called kings in the manner of the Canaanites. David settled in Hebron for a while, where, it is said, he planned the invasion of Jerusalem. In about 1000 BC he besieged the city; meeting stubborn resistance from the Jebusites, he entered it by a ruse, using the route from the Jihon spring, as we saw in Chapter 3.

The fall of Jerusalem, though very important, did not weaken the determination of the Canaanites to remain in their country, from the Amorite city of Dan in the north to the Amorite city of Hebron in the south. Beersheba and the Negev and Sinai were never inhabited by the Israelites.

"And the children of Israel dwelt among the Canaanites, Hittites and Amorites, and Perizzites, and Hivites, and Jebusites . . . and the children of Israel did evil in the sight of the Lord, and forgot the Lord their God, and served Baalim and the groves," (*Judges* 3: 5,7). Ba'alim, plural of Ba'al, were the gods of the Canaanites, to which many Israelites were ready to turn, wavering in their loyalty to Yahweh.

In general, the inhabitants of Palestine never submitted to the Hebrew invaders nor fully accepted them; they paid tribute only under duress, and in at least some instances it was the Hebrew that paid tribute to the Canaanites, (*Genesis* 49: 15).

On the verses from *Judges* quoted above, Sir John Glubb writes: "*Judges* 3: 5 puts the resulting situation in a nutshell. The Israelites lived among the Canaanites, the Hittites, the Amorites, the Perizzites, the Hivites and the Jebusites. They married the daughters of these peoples and gave their own daughters in marriage to their sons, and served their gods.

"The phrase 'they dwelt among them' may refer to the fact that they pitched their tents between the villages. It also implied that the Israelites were fewer than the people of the land. We can say that, in the United States, the Red Indians live among the white population, but we can not say that the whites live among the Red Indians, because the latter are fewer."[8]

NOTES

1 According to the Old Testament, Abraham was an Aramaean: an Arab.
2 It is curious that Ishmael, who was Isaac's brother and thirteen years his senior, does not appear in the Jewish or Zionist version of the promise. Ishmael, of course, is the traditional father of the Adnani Arabs.
3 Bright, *History of Israel*, pp. 172–3.
4 Pritchard, *The Ancient Near East*, p. 270.
5 F. F. Bruce, *Archaeology and Old Testament Study*, p. 6.
6 Kenyon, *Digging up Jericho*, p. 259.
7 Breasted, *Ancient Times*, pp. 200–1.
8 Glubb, *Peace in the Holy Land*, p. 52.

Chapter Eight

The Kingdom of David and Solomon

When David took Jerusalem and made it his capital, he did not extend its boundaries.[1] He was more of a warlord than a ruler, as was quite natural for a shepherd who became a warrior. He held Jerusalem, as it had been held before, under the aegis of Egypt, but he seems to have exercised some control well beyond the Kingdom of Jerusalem. At no time, however, did he rule the whole area of Palestine, and the plains and the coast in particular never fell within his sphere of influence.

David was succeeded by his son Solomon, whose government seems to have been better than his father's, although taxes were crushing and forced labour was extensively used. This was made necessary by the building of his palace or palaces, and by the erection of the Temple. As might have been expected, his harsh taxation policy produced unrest and almost led to disaster.

According to some sources, the Kingdom of Solomon reached as far as Aqaba, Sinai and Syria. It is highly unlikely that Solomon ruled "from Dan to Beersheba", as is stated in the famous verse of the Bible. In any case, he certainly did not rule the whole of Palestine, and, of course, the Israelites remained a small minority in the area.

The statistics cited in the Bible relating to numbers, ages, and events cannot, in the light of modern knowledge, be taken very seriously. Solomon may have been "wise", and indeed "wiser than all men" of his time, but the picture of scientific, philosophical and literary development, and of the king's wealth, must all be seen in perspective. "Forty thousand stalls of horses for his chariots and twelve thousand horsemen" seems excessive by any standards of the period.

It must be remembered that the books of the Old Testament were written by many writers over a period of several centuries, and were not completed until about 500 BC or even later. The discovery of the ancient and forgotten city of Ugarit has revealed that the Israelites borrowed considerably from other cultures. "Much of the best in Canaanite literature was adopted by the Hebrews and found its way into their sacred writings. This is especially true of the lyric pieces and borrowed sayings to be found in the Proverbs, the Psalms and the Song of Songs 'which is Solomon's', and in the mythical compositions embedded in Genesis and the Prophets."[2]

There can have been relatively few Israelites in Jerusalem. Kathleen Kenyon says: "It is quite evident that their number, especially in Jerusalem, must have been very limited, for the Jebusites never abandoned the city, and since the city's boundaries were not extended one may therefore suspect that only the official parts of Jerusalem were changed, and that the rest continued much as before."[3]

The Old Testament quotes the total number of Israelites in about 360 BC as being three-quarters of a million, but archaeological and historical analysis and the economic limitations of the country at the time indicate that this is a vastly exaggerated figure. It has been more reliably estimated that in Solomon's time the total population of Palestine was about a quarter of a million. The boundaries of the kingdoms of David and Solomon are variously delineated by later texts and by maps; during the existence of the kingdoms there can have been neither clear maps nor well-defined boundaries.

When Solomon died, Israelite sovereignty in the form of a united kingdom ended, after a period of only seventy years. As we have said, it had never been an absolute sovereignty nor had the Israelites been a wholly independent people.

Solomon's Temple

All the Canaanite tribes erected sanctuaries to house their gods. Each city-state had its temple in honour of the common deities,

A Canaanite Temple
This shows the ground-plan of the traditional temple. It was on this model that
Canaanites and Phoenicians built the temple for Solomon.
A: Vestibule   B: Holy place   C: Holy of Holies

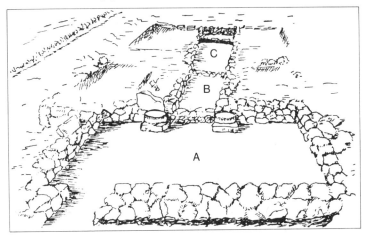

especially Ba'al. Worship had to be performed at sanctified sites;
the house of worship had to stand on an elevated place, reaching
upwards to the heavens where the gods had their true homes. In
Jerusalem, on Mount Ophel, there stood a large temple erected to
the Jebusites' chief god, Shalem.

The Israelites imitated Canaanite beliefs and practices,[4] and
later developed their own concept of monotheism. David began to
build a temple to Yahweh, to house the Tabernacle, which was
regarded as Yahweh's dwelling and which held the Ten Com-
mandments. He chose an elevation which was the property of
Arenna the Jebusite. But Yahweh did not encourage David to
build a permanent "home" in his honour, saying: "I have not dwelt
in any house ... even to this day, but have walked in a tent," (*II
Samuel* 7: 6). The reason for this was that the Israelites felt more
secure if their God moved with them. Nathan the prophet
informed David of Yahweh's will, and David stopped building the
temple. The reason given by the Old Testament is that David "had
been a man of war and had shed much blood" and had usurped the
Jebusite threshing-floor.

41

Solomon built the Temple, notwithstanding the fears and against the wishes of the people and the prophets. He built it on a raised floor according to Phoenician and Canaanite designs. A similar design can now be seen in the remains of the Canaanite towns of Beth-Shan, Hazan and Lachish. In the Old Testament may be found a detailed description of Solomon's Temple, from which it appears that a vestibule or porch opened into the main room or Holy Place (*Heikal*), and the Holy of Holies lay beyond this. In the Holy of Holies, which was unlit, there stood two large figures of cherubim, or winged sphinxes, carrying the Invisible God. In front of the Temple was an altar for burnt sacrifices. The dimensions of the Temple were twenty-five by eight metres.

Modern Israelis now claim that the Temple lies under the Muslim Mosque of Omar, the Dome of the Rock, but the fact is that the Temple was completely destroyed with nothing left to indicate even its location. The bases for present drawings of the sanctuary are the description in the Old Testament, "the discovery of a temple answering this description at Tel Taymat near Antioch,"[5] and the reconstructions by certain scholars. Some authorities believe that Solomon simply adapted a previous Jebusite temple which had also served as a fort.

The Temple was adjacent to the palaces which Solomon erected for his wives, who were allowed to practise their own religions; thus the way was open for many petty cults, "magic necromancy for the satisfaction of individual desires, side by side with the worship of Yahweh, as well as for the accommodation of strange gods of all sorts."[6]

Decline of the Kingdom

Religious and national disunity had begun among the Israelites in the days of David, and continued under Solomon, provoked by Solomon's manic extravagance and desire for personal aggrandisement, by internal conflicts, by the continued resistance of the native population and by the growth of Egypt's influence. Shortly after Solomon's death, the Egyptian pharaoh Shishanc occupied Jerusalem.

The kingdom was then divided into two, each bearing a considerable resemblance to the Canaanite city-states. The southern kingdom, which included Jerusalem and consisted of about a

Solomon's Temple
The temple was attached to Solomon's palace.

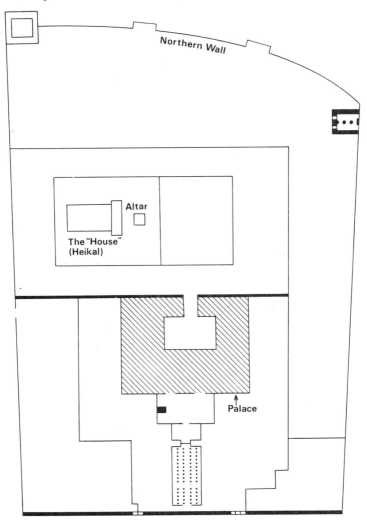

hundred square kilometres around the city, was called Judah; the northern kingdom, Israel, centred around modern Nablus. Neither had any influence outside its own confines, and both came under the sway of Assyria. Israel was conquered by Assyria in 722 BC, and Judah became a vassal of Babylon. In 586 BC Nebuchadnezzar, the king of Babylon, reacting to some defiance of his authority, besieged Jerusalem, burned the Temple, put an end to Jewish influence in the city and sent their leaders and many Israelite families into captivity in Babylon. Many other families fled to Egypt.

In Babylon, the Jews had time to study and to write, particularly on religious matters. It was there that Jewish ideas on monotheism were formulated and that the books of the Old Testament took shape. The composition and final collating of this body of literature took a long time, lasting almost to the beginning of the Christian era.

The effect of the Babylonian captivity was described by H. G. Wells thus: "The plain fact of the Bible narrative is that the Jews went to Babylon barbarians and came back civilised. They went a confused and divided multitude, with no national self-consciousness, they came back with an intense and exclusive national spirit."[7]

When Cyrus, King of Persia, ordered the return of the Jews of Babylonia to Jerusalem, the native inhabitants of the city strongly opposed the move, and for twenty years they succeeded in preventing the repair of the wall. Many of the prosperous Jews never returned to Jerusalem; they preferred to remain in Babylon.

NOTES

1 Kenyon, *Jerusalem, Excavating 3000 Years of History*, p. 50.
2 Hitti, *History of Syria*, pp. 114–15.
3 Kenyon, op. cit. p. 62.
4 G. Ernest Wright, *The Biblical Archaeological Reader I*, p. 173.
5 Note by Dr Baramki.
6 Isidore Epstein, *Judaism*, p. 37.
7 H. G. Wells, *Outline of History*, p. 265.

Chapter Nine

Subsequent Rulers of Jerusalem

The extension of Assyrian and Babylonian rule in Palestine, which ended the Israelite occupation of Jerusalem, was always pushed forward in the face of Egyptian influence, which sometimes succeeded in sharing the power. It is helpful to remember that the highway from Egypt at one end of the Fertile Crescent to Mesopotamia at the other ran through Palestine, and that the rise of one of these great empires was almost always at the expense of the other. Egypt attempted to extend its sphere of trade and influence to the east, while Assyria and Babylon were pushing from the opposite direction. It is clear that the aim of both was primarily commercial and that the security of trade-routes was their chief concern. Neither really wanted to occupy or to colonise land. Both had abundant resources of land, water, and man-power, and they preferred to govern through compliant native rulers who acted as their agents. Commerce and profit were the main aims. In general, the two peoples were of common stock, as was indicated by their frequent intermingling and by their languages, while their forms of government were usually of a kind that reflected their close ethnic relationship.

The brief period of Babylonian rule in Palestine was ended by the Persian invasion in 539 BC, when the Persian armies reached as far as Egypt. The permission given to the Jews to return to Jerusalem was an attempt to gain for Cyrus their assistance in the invasion of Egypt, and this help was in fact given. Some authors see a close parallel between Cyrus's action and the Balfour Declaration of 1917: both were motivated by political expediency rather than by any altruistic idealism.

In 323 BC the Greeks invaded Palestine and reached Jerusalem. Alexander's attempt to hellenise the country is well known, as is its lack of success. The religion, language, and customs of the Canaanites prevailed; not only was the influence of the warring Israelite community of little effect, but "some Jews made a determined attempt to hellenise Judaea . . . they saw the tiny Judaean state as a mere weak and helpless plaything . . . Its future security depended on its complete integration within the great Syro-Greek empire."[1]

During the period of Greek dominion, Judas Maccabaeus led a revolt against the Seleucids and against the Amorites who had regained power in Jerusalem, and he was able in 166 or 165 BC to establish an autonomous monarchical rule under the Seleucids. This uprising was said to have been the result of oppression by the Seleucids. Maccabaean government was weakened by internal divisions and was characterised by the worship of idols; it collapsed after a century.

The Greeks were succeeded by the Romans, who under the leadership of Pompey captured Jerusalem from the Maccabees in 63 BC. A period of semi-independent rule followed, under rulers who were for the most part vassals of Rome. The most prominent of these, Herod the Great, ruled from 40 BC to 4 BC. He was the son of an Edomite—an Arab—and although reputed to be half Maccabaean he leaned towards Rome rather than sharing the Jewish aspiration to rule Jerusalem. He did, however, build a temple far more magnificent than Solomon's, and partly secured Jewish recognition of it.

During the fairly early days of Roman rule, Jesus Christ appeared and proclaimed his Gospel. Although this could be regarded in a sense as a continuation and a development of Judaism, he was strongly opposed by the Jews, which led to his persecution, trial and execution. The attitude of the Canaanites and other local peoples was much less antagonistic, and many of them accepted the new religious message. The new Christians remained to form, with the pagans, the majority of the population both of Palestine and of Jerusalem.

It was the Roman general Titus who finally ended what little political significance remained to the Jews. He is said to have massacred most of the Jews of Jerusalem, plundered their property and demolished their temple and most of their buildings and monuments. The archaeological evidence of his destruction remains clear.

Palestine came under Greek and then Roman rule for nearly a millennium, yet the essential characteristics of the basically Arab inhabitants were not appreciably affected. Political power over the area passed from Rome to Byzantium at the beginning of the fourth century AD, and ended in AD 637, when a new flood of Arab immigrants came out of the heart of Arabia into the Fertile Crescent. This time they came flying the banner of a new religion, Islam. The Byzantine armies, which outnumbered the Arabs, put up fierce resistance and several great battles were fought, notably on the Yarmuk River. Many of the inhabitants of Palestine, Christian and Pagan alike, sided with the newcomers and helped to put an end at last to foreign rule.

Omar, the second Muslim Caliph, entered Jerusalem at the invitation of its inhabitants. He was one of the very few men in history to capture Jerusalem without shedding a drop of human blood. In his famous charter he issued the terms of surrender. The fact that these terms were concluded with Sophronius, the Christian Patriarch, indicates that the small Jewish rump that remained in the city had little importance.

Before Omar reached Jerusalem, he was aware of the Nabataean Arabs who had established Petra, of the Ghassanid Arabs of Hawran, and of the Manatherah of Mesopotamia. He knew Jerusalem as the place from which, according to Islam, his Prophet Mohammed had flown up to heaven on his night journey. It was also the Prophet's *qiblah* (direction of prayer) to which he turned his face when praying.

From the time when Muslim rule was established in 637 AD, the Arabs unquestionably formed the majority of the inhabitants of the Holy City, and until 1517 AD it was Arab rulers who governed it for most of the time, apart from relatively brief periods of Turkish and Crusader domination.

NOTE

1 Isidore Epstein, *Judaism*, p. 91.

Chapter Ten

The Continuity of Arab Settlement in Jerusalem

There is no difficulty in showing the racial link between the twentieth-century Arabs of Palestine and Jerusalem and the Arab Muslims who arrived in 638 AD with the Muslim conquest of the country, or with their kindred in subsequent movements. The supporting historical and archaeological evidence is abundant and relatively recent.

When, however, we attempt to study the racial links between the Arabs who came to the country during the wave of the Islamic conquests and afterwards, and those Jebusites and Canaanites who had inhabited the country during the distant millennia referred to earlier, we must bear in mind one feature which was characteristic of Palestine and Jerusalem and which did not exist in Egypt or Mesopotamia.

Geographical and other conditions militated against the emergence in Palestine of large monarchies or great empires. Jerusalem was only one example of a city-state generally ruled by successive *sheikhs* (chiefs) or *melks* (kings). No unification of their different city-states, nor even a federation of significant size, ever came into existence. The Canaanite city-states remained independent and politically separate from one another.

Clearly it is not surprising that these relatively small communities did not preserve lists of local chiefs going back for thousands of years. But this need not prevent us from tracing the history of the tribes and the peoples themselves. The presence and the continued existence of the peoples in the land are of more

48

fundamental importance than mere catalogues of rulers, especially if those rulers were foreigners. The stock to which the Arabs of ancient Jerusalem and Palestine belonged always formed the overwhelming majority of the population.

Even when they were resisting invasion, the city-states were not united. Only in very rare cases they did join together in efforts to repulse an attack. The parallel with the ancient Greeks is obvious. One of these cases was the union of Jerusalem with several neighbouring cities which successfully blocked Hebrew invasions of Jerusalem under Joshua and other generals for more than two centuries.

Throughout the periods under discussion, historic and prehistoric, the inhabitants of the cities of Palestine were basically Arab. If their ratio to other incoming inhabitants varied, this was never enough to change the general balance of the population, and in any case would have been less marked in the villages and desert communities than in the cities. As is always the case with foreign invasion or infiltration, it was the cities that were the main objectives of the incoming peoples, who underwent a process of assimilation by the native population. The Arab race, for various reasons, has over the centuries developed a special aptitude for absorbing foreign peoples and imparting its culture to them.

In this respect the history of Jerusalem is simple. It started as a Jebusite settlement, and the original name was retained. The Canaanite language was spoken by the majority of the inhabitants of Jerusalem until about 400 BC, when the Aramaic language, also a dialect of Arabic, took over. Aramaic remained the *lingua franca* until modern Arabic was introduced by the Arab Muslim conquest and this is still used today. During the period of the Ottoman rule, which lasted for 400 years, the effect of the Turkish language was negligible. The British mandate introduced English and Hebrew as official languages alongside Arabic, but Arabic remained the main language. The effect of English and Hebrew was also negligible as far as Arab culture and social conventions were concerned.

The Arab peoples and tribes displayed little desire for change and adaptation, but their effect on the peoples who came into contact with them has been marked. To the Israelites they gave their language as well as other cultural characteristics. To the Turks the Arabs gave their religion, their alphabet and the high proportion of Arabic in the Turkish vocabulary. The Arabs always showed a tendency to develop cultures which acted as nurseries for other civilisations.

The continuity of Arab settlement in Jerusalem and Palestine has formed the subject of special studies by many foreign scholars. Frances E. Newton concluded that it is the Arabs and not the Jews who have had the constant, uninterrupted and continuous historical connection with Palestine. She quotes Sir James Frazer as saying: "The Arab-speaking peasants of Palestine are the descendants of the pagan tribes which dwelt there before the Israelite invasions, and have always clung to the soil ever since, being submerged but never destroyed by each successive wave of conquest which has swept over the land."[1] It is well established that the peasants of the country remained by and large in a majority among the population.

These conclusions have been corroborated by Mrs E. A. Finn, who lived in Jerusalem for a period of almost twenty years. As wife of the British Consul she studied the Palestinian peasantry, particularly around Jerusalem. Although Mrs Finn uses the Bible as her major source, she concludes that "there is no difficulty on the score of habit, custom or religion in our way. None of all these need prevent us from regarding the *fellaheen* (peasants) as being relics of the ancient Canaanites. Neither does it seem to us that the fact of their speaking the Arabic language offers any difficulty."[2] Mrs Finn states further that there has been no evidence, archaeological or otherwise, to show that the original inhabitants of Palestine had left the country either voluntarily or by forcible expulsion, or had ever been annihilated *in situ*, at any period of their existence. She underlines the enormous influence wielded by the Arab population on the Jewish community through intermarriage and by the use of Arabic. Even "Nehemiah complains that the languages of their heathen masters were spoken by the children, who could not understand the Jews' tongue."[3]

When the Muslim Arabs entered Jerusalem and Palestine they mixed easily with the existing peoples, most of whom eventually adopted the new religion of Islam. The native peoples, according to Mrs Finn, were the Canaanites, the Jebusites, the Amorites, the Hivites, the Perizzites and the Hittites. She adds: "It is of these five nations that we have been more particularly speaking as in all probability still forming the rural population of Palestine."[4]

Mrs Finn ends her study with the following words: "In the foregoing pages we argued in favour of the probability that the present rural population of Palestine, the Arab *fellaheen*, are descendants of the ancient Canaanite nations. First, because five of those nations continued to exist in the land until the Christian era, and cannot have been annihilated or driven out since. Secondly, because the *fellaheen* are apparently aboriginal people and there is no tradition or record to show that they are anything else. Thirdly, because many customs of the Canaanites prohibited in the law of Moses still exist as customs of the *fellaheen*. Fourthly, because they have preserved the ancient geographical names. And lastly, because there appear to be customs among them derived from the Israelites."[5]

We may therefore take as established facts the statements which form the basis of the whole thesis: Jerusalem was founded by Arabs; throughout its existence they never abandoned it, and they always remained the basic population. They ruled the city for longer than all the invaders, and when the invaders were expelled or had become assimilated the original inhabitants invariably repossessed the city.

The period between 1000 BC, when David conquered Jerusalem, and 1948, when the new state of Israel was proclaimed on the strength of an unlawful decision by the UN, is approximately 3000 years. During these three millennia the Israelites ruled Jerusalem for only 70 years, a period which was subject in various degrees to Phoenician influence on the one hand and to Egyptian rule on the other. The two Jewish sub-kingdoms of Judaea and Samaria were no more politically important than the other city-states of the time in Hebron, Megiddo, Gaza and elsewhere. Jewish rule in Jerusalem lasted to the end of the Kingdom of Judaea in 587 BC. The Maccabaean control of Jerusalem gave local autonomy under the overall aegis of the Seleucids, which lasted for about 100 years.

An objective historian cannot overlook a contrast here. We know of no claim to Palestine or any part of it by the Persians, who later ruled Jerusalem for an uninterrupted period of 200 years; nor by the Greeks, whose continuous rule lasted for 300 years; nor by the Romans, who stayed for about 700 years. Yet we find the Zionists claiming an "historical right" to Jerusalem and Palestine, and, presumably, to other Arab lands. The Arabs do not claim any such right in Spain, where they lived and ruled for a period of 800 years, leaving behind the legacy of a magnificent and original civilisation.

The period of uncontested Arab habitation and rule in and around Jerusalem and Palestine covers at least 8000 years. Even if only the thirteen centuries of Arab rule in Palestine from the Muslim conquest onwards were considered, then the Arabs' right to the land could not conceivably be contested.

Sir James Frazer comes to the following interesting conclusion: "If extravagant claims drawn upon dim antiquity provide title deeds in Palestine then it is the Arabs who have the really extravagant and wholly ancient claim, and their right to these strange title deeds is as unquestionable as their right to the true deeds proceeding from their current thirteen centuries of occupation."[6]

These facts overwhelm the Zionists themselves, and as a result they fall back on overbearing arrogance. Nahum Goldmann, the president of the World Jewish Congress and former president of the World Zionist Organisation, said:

"The Jews might have had Uganda, Madagascar, and other places for the establishment of a Jewish Fatherland, but they want absolutely nothing except Palestine; not because the Dead Sea water by evaporation can produce five trillion dollars' worth of metalloids and powdered metal, not because the subsoil of Palestine contains twenty times more petroleum than all the combined reserves of the two Americas, but because Palestine constitutes the veritable centre of world political power, the strategic centre for world control."

NOTES

1 Frances E. Newton, *Fifty Years in Palestine*, p. 5.
2 E. A. Finn, *Palestine Peasantry*, p. 46.
3 ibid., p. 43.
4 ibid., p. 48.
5 ibid., p. 94.
6 Frazer, *Palestine, the Reality*, p. 12.

Bibliography

ALBRIGHT, W. F. *The Archaeology of Palestine* (Penguin Books) London, 1967

THOMAS, D. W. ed. *Archaeology and Old Testament Study* (Clarendon Press) Oxford, 1967

BREASTED, J. H. *Ancient Times* (Ginn & Co.) Aylesbury, 1960

BRIGHT, JOHN *History of Israel* (SCM Press) London, 1967

COLE, SONIA *Races of Man* (British Museum) London, 1965

Encyclopaedia Britannica Article on Jerusalem, 1963

EPSTEIN, ISIDORE *Judaism* (Penguin Books) London, 1967

FINN, E. A. *Palestine Peasantry* (Marshal Press) London, 1923

GLUBB, JOHN BAGOT *Peace in the Holy Land* (Hodder & Stoughton) London, 1971

HITTI, PHILIP *History of the Arabs* 9th edn. (Macmillan) New York, 1968

—— *History of Syria* 2nd edn. (Macmillan) London, 1957

HOADE, FR. EUGENE *Guide to the Holy Land* (Franciscan Press) Jerusalem, 1960

KENYON, KATHLEEN M. *Digging up Jericho* (Benn) London, 1957

—— *Jerusalem, Excavating 3000 Years of History* (Thames & Hudson) London, 1967

NEWTON, FRANCES E. *Fifty Years in Palestine* (Coldharbour Press) England, 1948

NOTH, MARTIN *The History of Israel* (A. & C. Black) London, 1960

PRITCHARD, JAMES B. *The Ancient Near East* (Princeton and Oxford University Press) USA and London, 1958

WELLS, H. G. *The Outline of History* (Cassell) London, 1920

WINKLER, HUGO *The History of Babylonia and Syria*, trans. James A. Craig, New York, 1907

WRIGHT, G. ERNEST *The Biblical Archaeological Reader 1* (Anchor Books, Doubleday) New York, 1961

ZEIDAN, GEORGI *The Arabs before Islam* (Al-Hilal Press) Cairo, 1922 (Arabic)

Chronological Table

BC

9000   Early migration to Fertile Crescent from Arabian Peninsula.
Habitation at the site of Jericho.
Building of Jericho.

5000   Amorite migrations. (c.4500)

4000   Jebusites build Jerusalem.
Major influx of Arab tribes, including Canaanites. (c.3500)
Development of Alphabetical writing. (c.3500)

3000   Further Amorite immigration.
Canaanite Jericho built. (c.3000)

2000   Gathering of "Habiru" tribes: Abraham's journey from Ur.
Further immigration from the Peninsula. (c.1500)
Influx of Hittites. (c. 1750)
Influx of Hyksos. (c.1700)
Influx of Philistines. (c.1200)

1000   David captures Jerusalem.
Solomon's kingdom divided.
Shishanc of Egypt captures Jerusalem. (c.935)
Jebusite rule returns to Jerusalem. (c.895)
Jewish kingdom of Samaria ends. (c.722)
Jewish kingdom of Judaea ends. (c.597)
Assyrian and Babylonian conquest. (c.730–539)
Persian conquest. (c.539–332)
Greek conquest. (c.363–32)
Roman conquest and occupation. (c.63 BC–AD 637)

AD   Muslim Arabs enter from Arab Peninsula. (c.AD 638)

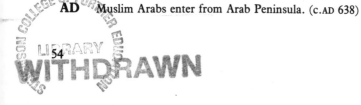